Essence of Black Beauty

A Collection of Inspirational, Romantic and Erotic Poetry

by

Syneeda Penland

Adeenys Publishing,
Publisher Since 2015

ISBN-10:   1-942863-01-2
ISBN-13:   978-1-942863-01-4

Published in the United States

Cover Design by Sy'needa Penland

This book is dedicated to GOD, my beloved mother Wanda, my grandmother Ruth and my late father Richard. I will always love and treasure each of you with all my heart.

ACKNOWLEDGMENT

I would like to thank my family, friends and closest spiritual advisors for their love and support during my most trialing times in the military. A heartfelt thanks for their patience and devotion during my transition in regaining my independence and spiritual freedom. I am deeply honored and thankful to God for blessing me with remarkable gifts and the ability to touch through to a person's soul, to help soothe their spirit with my inspirational and sensual words of poetry. I will always treasure my gifts and use them for the preservation of humanity.

Contents

PART II: LOVE, HOPE AND HAPPINESS

PART III: HAIKUS

PART IV: BLACK HEAVEN EROTICA

I Shall Not Falter

A Blessing from God

When our *Heavenly Father*
blessed me with life,
he adorned me for his wife.

He planted my seed
upon *Mother Earth*,
nine months later
my Mother gave birth.

I would soon become
one of his most precious *Black Rose*,
within each of my pedals
my story is told.

My bud is my center,
it holds my truth,
it is within my stem
which connects my root.

For I am one of many flowers
Father God planted upon *Mother* Earth,
He added me to *her* canvas upon my birth.

Each year I grow one inch taller
so I can be closer
to our *Heavenly Father*.

Afro

I saw a *Sistah* at a restaurant the other day,
She was wearing an *Afro*, an Angela Davis,
Foxy Brown - 1970's looking *Afro*.
This *Sistah* certainly knew how to wear her *Afro*.

It was all picked out, full and thick,
And a little rough around the edges.
Her hair and all its sheen
Truly defined her blackness.

It was *exotic!*
It was *sexy!*
It was *beautiful!*
It was *strong!*
It was *powerful!*

This *Sistah* exuded just the right attitude
To wear her *Afro*. She was casually well-dressed,
Barely wearing any make-up, just a little eyeliner,
Mascara and lipstick, that's it.

Her flawless beauty was so radiant,
I was captivated by the
Essence of her Black Beauty.

It was mature- not aged.
Strong- yet feminine.
Warm, intelligent and compassionate.
Like *Mother Earth*.

America

After centuries of being denied access to our history,
African-American history is no longer a mystery.

After being kidnapped from *our* homeland,
told false promises of being returned to our origin,
America is now home to me.

Holding her torch, the *Statue of Liberty*,
a symbol of freedom- promises of *false hope*
that in *America* you will no longer feel choked.

Strangled by shackles around your feet and hands,
you've landed on the shores of the so-called,
"Promise Land."

Many centuries ago, these shores laid home
to my *other* ancestors who were *free* to roam
up and down the shores of America's creeks.

Native American Indian's land
and natural resources
is what explorers would seek.

This land of the *West*
is what explorers called *"the New World,"*
soon became home for other nations to explore.

America is now considered home to many races;
Black, white, red, yellow- many brown faces.

America, America, land of liberty;
America, America, will I,
on *our* land ever be free?!

A R I I U S

African...   A descendant of the *Motherland*

Roots...   Our origin, our heritage;
Our ties to *Mother Africa* (Ah-*free*-kah)

Is...   Our *purpose* for *living*

In...   Our spirit, mind, body and soul

Us...   All *GOD's* children

Black in America

Berated

   Labeled

      Accused

         Chastised

            Killed

            Incarcerated   **N**eglected

Admired

   Mocked

      Exploited

         Ridiculed

            Insulted

               Criticized

                  Achievers

Black Pearls of Wisdom

Deep inside the dark pit of the abyss
I let out a loud scream; crying out to God,
"Lord, what does all of this really mean?!"

I've traveled the earth;
40 days, 40 nights, 40 years
since my birth,
only to experience a re-birth,
to awaken from a curse.

My mind, my body, my spirit
held in captivity;
I've arisen from the *pit of hell*
only to discover all the lies
that's been told to me.

I am but a stem, a cell,
once-twice divided
from the seeds of Mother Earth,
two souls intertwined upon my birth.

Living in one body,
conjoined at the head;
one soul represents the living,
the other- the dead.

At the ripen age of adulthood
what am I now to believe,
"The ancient story that humans
are descendants of *only* Adam and Eve?"

The Roman Catholic religion
dates back for *only* 2000 years,
yet for centuries their lies
have been cemented inside our ears.

Some say wars on religion
is a sign of Armageddon,

I say it's God's way of unveiling
all the secrets that's been hidden.

I don't like to argue my belief
or disbelief in religion,
but connected to our minds,
our bodies and our souls
is where the truth is really hidden.

The human heart is magnetically charged
by God's *spirit* called *life*.
God shines his Glory, the Sun,
onto Mother Earth, his wife.

We are all *Star Seeds*, human *Angels*,
sent here to protect Mother Earth.
Arriving from the deep abyss
of God's *Black Heaven*,
far beyond the reaches of man.
The truth of our existence
man has yet to understand.

Mother Earth has become restless
from all the chaos caused by man,
his threats of nuclear war;
seeking to destroy her precious land.

As a *Fire Child*...
I see...
I hear...
I feel...
The echo vibrations of Mother Earth's cry.
She's asking us to worship her in *Peace*,
before mankind is called forth to die.

The stories of *his* sins are outlined
in *his* Holy book. Tales of how *man*
came to destroy *himself*
and how long it took.

His-story is a lesson learned
that is **not** to be repeated!

As *Mother Earth*
gets closer to our *Father Sun*,
she'll start to get very heated.

Her fiery lust for her protector
is what is really needed,
to bleed out *hate* from the souls of man,
leaving the tears of her daughters
to finally nourish her precious land, again.

Peace and Love will save us in the end!

Cascading Falls

Like one of the *Seven Wonders* of the world
for all to see, the beauty of cascading falls
flows majestically.

Pouring down like thundering rain,
crashing against my windowpane.
Forbidding rays of light to shine through.

A gloomy, dreary mist,
wish all was blue
and as beautiful as you.

Coming Full Circle

(Dedicated to the memory of my father)

Does death immortally bond us
or does our love fade away?
Will thoughts of you always be with us
with each passing day?

Death is a strange thing,
oftentimes you don't know how to feel.
A feeling of numbness is first felt,
while accepting the truth
everything around you seems surreal.

What's left are the memories of your smile
and the words that you have spoken.
The many ways you touched our hearts,
your memories become a token.

Your generosity and your kindness,
always showing that you care,
those who truly knew you
could count on you to always be there.

No matter how you chose to live your life;
experiencing many trials and tribulations.
You maintained your faith in GOD,
in the end, receiving his affirmation.

Through *your* life's journey;
finally *coming full circle*,
you remained grounded in your beliefs.
With each passing word you spoke,
you never showed discern of disbelief.

It was your wish that we celebrate this occasion
to always remember you at your very best.
Now *you* say farewell to all of us
as we lay you down to rest.

I stand here today to proudly accept the torch
of your legacy, the memories of your kind spirit
and caring ways will forever remain inside of me.

If I may speak on behalf of my siblings
as we proudly say:
"I am my Father's Daughter!"
"I am my Father's Son!"

Dear Father, it is *your* legacy
we *will* continue to carry on.
We love you and may you *Rest in Peace*!

Compassion

Tear drops fall
from your sadden eyes,
stricken by grief of a loved one
who recently died.

Gently, I cradle your fragile hands,
placing them in the warmth of mine.
I lay your head on my shoulders
and close my eyes,
I *make a wish...*

Wishing I could turn back
the hands of time,
to erase away the pain
from your grieving heart.
To fill your life with happier days
filled with laughter;
before your life was torn apart.

Turning back the hands of time
to blissful days filled with cheer;
before your world was shattered
into tiny little pieces;
before your eyes drowned in tears.

When I think about your sorrow,
I wish I could erase away your pain
for a much brighter tomorrow.

When I look up at the stars tonight
I will make a wish...

A promise from GOD is,
"Everything will be alright!"

Country Gone, City Girl

Much too often I refer to myself
as a *"Country Gone, City Girl."*
Severing my roots from the South
in pursuit to travel and explore the world.

My dreams and aspirations
to pursue my goals
took me far away from home.

I traveled to many cities,
and experienced many cultures
around the world.
From the Arabian Seas,
to the Pacific Islands,
to Africa, Asia, Spain,
Italy, Greece and Rome.

This ol' *Country* gal has gotten tired
from the hustle and bustle of city life,
so I'm headed back home-
deep down South to settle down.

I'm gonna' find myself
a *Good ol' Southern Beau*
to ultimately become his wife.

Dance a Song of Celebration

Let us rejoice in song
to a jubilee, a celebration.
Sending our spirits in flight
as we dance in song,
commemorating
the unity of our nations.

No longer will we be oppressed
by pain and sorrow from our past.
Let us join together by uplifting our voices
and sing a song that will forever last.

No more endless tears or blood-shed
from years of spiritual annihilation.
Let us celebrate and commemorate
the peaceful unity of our *Nations*.

Dangerous Playground of Love

Like children on the playground
playing on the swings and in the sand.
Always yellin' and playing games
while kissing and holding hands.

Playing hop-scotch, jumping rope,
sometimes hide and seek.
Even red-light and green-light,
never playing fair, always have to peek.

As we grow older
we reminisce in laughter
with thoughts of how we played.
The games we learned back then,
as adults, we continue to play.

As a child, we played them
each and every day.
Mastered them skillfully,
rehearsed them play by play.

In a relationship, cat and mouse
is simply hide and seek.
Ya' always chasin',
Ya' always lyin',
Ya' always have to peek.

You start by asking questions,
then sneak and check emails,
you'll even stalk your mate.
Once you are caught
it's their turn to win,
so you'll begin to *"playa"* mate.

The game becomes more childish
just like a playground crush.
Excited by the thrill of the game,
love is lost, it fades to lust.

The passion is fueled by keeping score
of who wins or loses.
When the game becomes boring
the more *playas* you'll choose.

You begin to change the rules
to appease your sexual greed.
The new rules are written
to satisfy *your* selfish needs.

As we grow older,
we may never escape
this *dangerous playground of love*,
by never maturing to fully develop
and experience true love.

This playground is dangerous,
it's filled with germs and deadly diseases.
The more who are playing
comes more lies, more sex
and more STDs.

Dawning of a New Day

Up against a mountain,
I stand tall.
I've weathered the storm,
I fought them all.

They gathered their armies
and slandered my name,
forcing me into hiding
to avoid any shame.

I've suffered pain and agony
while living in fear,
always running and hiding
the closer they drew near.

Tired of feeling helpless
from not submitting to Da' Man,
I got down on my knees
and prayed to the LORD for *His* plan.

I donned *GOD's* armor,
preparing for the next battle of war.
Still faced with adversity,
I was determined to settle the score.

My enemies stood before me,
their evil words pierced my shield.
Yet I never surrendered to the wickedness
while in the sorcerer's field.

I broke away from my silence
and cried out from the mountain top,
"Demanding *PEACE*, for this war to stop!"

The arrogance of their egos
forbid them to quit.
To take responsibility for their actions,
they will never admit.

My enemies would rather live in sin
and carry their lies to their grave,
rather than submitting to the LORD
for their souls to be saved.

LORD, this victory is yours,
I'm forever blessed to have served,
as one of your soldiers
remaining fully committed to your word!

Dear Father

(Dedicated to the memory of my father)

You once called me your '*little Rose*',
I was the sunshine of your eye.
Your teachings taught me
to remain centered, grounded.
Throughout my life I've remained humble,
always will until I die.

You were a man of strength and courage,
I obeyed the wisdom of your every word.
Whenever faced with adversity, your teachings
taught me to never get discouraged.

Your light shines down from heaven
to always be the beacon in my life;
long after your spirit transcended to heaven,
well into the afterlife.

Dear Father, thank you for your care,
your love and affection. Most of all,
thank you for your words of wisdom
which have always protected me
from pain, sorrow and affliction.

Dear Grandmother
(Dedicated to my grandmother)

I recall as a little girl,
you taught me right from wrong.
Your words of wisdom stood steadfast,
like a cadence guiding me along.

As I traveled through many hills and valleys,
my temperament stood strong.
I never fell out of step
as I danced to the rhythm
of your sweet song.

Righteousness is what you taught me,
to never compromise my values
just to get along. Even at the final hour
of my misfortune, I felt you in my spirit,
I was never alone.

Dear Mother
(Dedicated to my mother)

I have felt alone, like a child
secured within your womb.
In complete isolation
from the rest of the world,
yearning to be awakened
from my tomb.

Your spirit, your love,
your passion for life
co-exists within my soul.
Yet I've felt abandoned, alone;
lost in the wilderness,
isolated in the cold.

For weeks my mind could not fathom
what we thought would be the inevitable,
fearing what would become.
My eyes could not bear
seeing you lying there, *helpless*.

You're my *Heart!*
You're my *Soul!*
You're my *Mom!*

It was painful for me to leave your bedside,
more painful to let go of your hand.
There was nothing I could do or say
but pray and make amends.

I've carried the guilt of decisions I've made,
not adhering to your advice.
Ignoring you at times with *rage* and *fury*,
my disobedience caused strife.

When the news finally reached me,
learning of what you'd succumb;

I was *motionless*, my body felt *lifeless*,
as I shivered, I felt completely numb.

Years of my existence
began to flash before my eyes,
I got down on my knees to pray,
begging the LORD to save *you*,
'Take me instead', I screamed, "Let me die!"

I couldn't imagine taking another breath
without knowing if you'll be alright.
I couldn't rid hearing the sound
of your sweet voice,
or seeing the image of your beautiful face,
what a lovely sight!

Arriving to be by your bedside,
I embraced the warmth of your gentle hand,
suddenly I felt the *Spirit* of the LORD move me
as I whispered into your ear to tell you *His* plan.

When I closed my eyes to pray,
I held on to your hand real tight.
Overcome by *His* power to heal you,
He assured me you'll be alright.

Holding on to your hand
in the mist of the storm,
I didn't want to let it go.
I'd regressed back to a helpless child,
once lost, not knowing which way to go.

It was the LORD's plan that has guided me,
giving you, *Mother* the courage to see it through.
He has a plan for all of us, GOD's children,
Dear Mother, even you!

Decisions

Sitting here numb,
my thoughts are frozen in time.
Wondering how did I get here?
Stop! Let me rewind.

Retracing my steps,
revisiting each decision I've made,
subsequently sitting here pondering,
"For a better life would I trade?"

The cost of *Freedom* is priceless,
no more conforming to the norm.
My life is now my own,
no longer will they bring me harm.

To be a prisoner of an institution
filled with lies and deceit,
those wearing the uniform of top brass,
from our pockets they cheat.

As a proud American
it was an honor to have served,
defending our country,
'*A Free Nation*' is what we deserve.

Yet I did not go along to get along,
I stand behind my conviction;
remaining fully committed to the LORD,
to His word, His *powerful* intervention!

Departure

Letting go of the baggage in my life,
Free from stress and worry,
No more arguing,
No more strife.

Getting rid of the weight
That once held me down.
Gaining new footage,
Now on solid ground.

Departing from an old life,
Headed on a course for something new.
Looking forward to new horizons,
New beginnings, peace and solitude.

Don't Give Up

Stand up.
Stand tall.
Fight for what you believe in.
Don't give up!

When you feel like you can't go on,
Get down on your knees and pray.
Ask the *LORD* for His guidance,
He'll guide you on your way.

Remain true to your convictions
By always having faith in the *LORD*.
Listen to His guidance,
Count on Him to steer the way.

Don't be discouraged
By the devil's evil ways,
He'll gather his army
To try to lead you astray.

Continue to fight for what you believe in
By always giving praise to the *LORD*.
He'll protect you through your battles,
He'll never lead you astray.

Like the *Foot Prints in the Sand*,
He'll carry your weight.
The weight of all your worries,
To ease your pain away.

You are a child of *GOD*
In need of His care,
He will never forsake you
And will always be there.

Essence of Black Beauty

As time has changed
so have generations of our times,
leaving intriguing tales
and mysteries of our past,
I search for answers, seeking to find...

I seek to explore the *Essence*
which defines the mystery
of our hidden taboos,
depicted by false labels and stereotypes;
shamelessly dictating all that we do.

Have we allowed these labels to shame us
from vicious acts exploited in the past?
Allowing this fear to still haunt us,
how much longer will it last?

No one put us on a pedestal
to be portrayed as delicate and pure;
instead, curious of the '*Essence of our Black Beauty*',
strongly desired by those seeking to endure.

To fulfill the desires of their fantasies,
to strip us of all that was once pure.
Planting a seed to become *nameless,*
scarring our souls leaving us *shameless*
of brutal acts- never *painless*!

This scar, passed on to each generation,
left never to be discussed yet complete annihilation
from the history of the heritage of *"African Queens."*

This heritage, so enriched by the beauty of her land,
cradled in the *essence* of her bosom, her jewels
and all her riches are strongly desired by man.

No longer will we be haunted
by the mystery of our hidden taboos,

which *defaces our heritage*
and wrongfully defines what is true.

For being *Black,* defines the beauty
that lies deep within our skin.
Either at its *purest* or *mixed* with other,
combining such a *beautiful* blend.

To all my sistahs of color,
"Be proud of who you are!"
Show the world that you are able
to lift the taboos, stereotypes
and many false labels.

Look in the mirror
and inhale your beauty.
Embrace it!
And say out loud,
with a wink of an eye of acceptance, say
"I'm Black!"
"I'm Beautiful!"
"I'm Proud!"

Fighting to Survive

Catch me, I'm falling.
Protect me before I hit the ground.
My mind's goin' round and round,
On their walls I pound.
Their walls will come tumbling down,
'Cause *I'm a fighter*, hear my cry*!*

They tried to attack my character
And my pride, what I possess inside.
I fought back like I knew I should,
They never thought I could
Stand my ground.
On their walls I pound,
Determined to hold my ground,
I will not back down!

The mighty roar of a *Lion*,
Out loud *I* cry!
I will hold my head high,
High above the clouds
From the highest mountain top,
I will not give up, I will not stop,
'Cause *I'm a fighter*, fighting to survive!

Forgiveness

Hidden behind a mask,
your face I dare reveal.
Will you tear my heart into pieces,
my identity will you steal?

To practice you is an art,
one I've yet to master.
The wrath your kin left behind
was an emotional disaster.

Hate is your brother,
human kind he does not pity.
He dwells within each of us,
his nickname is *"Misery."*

He's afraid to be left alone,
afraid he'll be forgotten.
His stench is awfully foul,
his soul is dead and rotten.

Peace is your sister,
she forever shines her light.
If you look up at the stars at night
you'll see her heart shine bright.

Protected by their mother *Earth*,
Love is her name.
Embarrassed by her son *Hate*,
she lives quietly in shame.

Forgiveness is your father,
he'll rescue you from pain.
He'll deliver you from your past,
he'll embrace you with his name.

He'll wash away your sins,
a new life he will restore,
call out to him in your time of need,
he'll forgive you now and forever more.

Friendship

Friendship is an honest
and trusted relationship,
that can stand the test of time.
It's a bond, a covenant,
you never cross the line.

It's time shared with others,
in both good times and in bad.
It's showing others that you truly care
and comfort them when they're sad.

It's when someone accepts *you*
for whom *you* are.
They will never disrespect *you*
or try to change who they truly are.

True friendship is hard to come by,
it's when you *genuinely* give from your heart.
You will never let anything come between you
and nothing can tear it apart.

Ghetto Swagga

Leaps and bounds,
so astound,
life profound.

We all have the ability to make it,
don't let anybody try and take it!
My ground is solid,
can't nobody shake it!

Like an earthquake's aftershock,
try to break my spirit,
I think not!

Like a volcano eruption,
my center is burning hot.
Flowing like lava.

My foundation is solid,
solid as a rock.
Can't nobody break it,
shake it or take it!

Don't get it twisted
or misunderstood,
I may sound proper
but I'm straight from the hood.

Match that with several college degrees,
don't ever try to take my shit
and don't ever try to fuck with me!

'Cause when you do
nothing else matters,
you'll feel the wrath of my
'Ghetto Swagga!'

Happiness

What I *yearn* for…
What I *search* for…
What I *live* for…

Deep within my soul,
For what makes me whole…
What makes me complete.

Can this way of life fulfill me?
Give me what I want,
Make me complete?

Is it I, who needs to define
What validates me?
What makes me whole,
What makes me complete?

I live my life from dawn 'til dusk,
Days routinely- circular with no end.
These rings spinning round and round,
My life impound, I must rebound!

I search aimlessly for the truth,
For what lies deep within my soul,
For what makes me whole,
What makes me complete.

I search for joy and laughter,
For the feeling to one day allow me
To define the true meaning of
'Who *I* Am!'

For this feeling of *happiness*,
Do I have to be someone who's liked?
Someone who's known to be filled with delight?
Someone who is *complete*?
Someone who is *whole*?

Yet I feel empty,
Like something is missing
From deep within my soul.

I yearn for the feeling,
I yearn for the day,
When I am *complete!*
When I am *whole!*
When I am *happy*,
All day!

Humble

The air is still,
    The sea is calm.
To render my will
    I will succumb
To the virtue of my soul,
    By remaining humble
To my spirit,
    Through the years
As I grow old.

I Am My Mother's Daughter

When I wake up every morning
And look in the mirror to see my face,
    I realize...
I am My Mother's Daughter!

When I look at my smooth brown skin,
My kinky hair and the twinkle in my eyes,
    I realize...
I am My Mother's Daughter!

When I notice the strut in my walk,
My sassy style, or at times the tone in my voice,
    I realize...
I am My Mother's Daughter!

When I exude the courage, strength and wisdom,
To get me through hard times,
    I realize...
I am My Mother's Daughter!

No matter how many times we try to change ourselves
Or deny who we truly are, we can never change
Or deny our heritage, which is *You,* who I see in *Me.*

I am truly blessed to be, *"My Mother's Daughter!"*

I Can Always Count on You

LORD, I come to you in prayer,
I come to you on bended knee.
I've always known that you'll be there,
By my side in time of need.

Time and time again
When I needed someone,
When I needed a friend,
LORD, you answered my prayers.

You comforted my soul
By showing me that
I can always count on you.

LORD, I come to you in prayer,
I come to you on bended knee.
I've always known that you'll be there,
By my side in time of need.

Time and time again
When I was lost and weary,
In need of a friend,
LORD, you answered my prayers.

You never left my side,
You were always there,
I can always count on you.

LORD, I come to you in prayer,
I come to you on bended knee.
I've always known that you'll be there,
By my side in time of need.

When I'm lost and confused,
Don't know what to do;
You'll answer my prayers,
You'll show me what to do.

You will always be there,
I can always count on you.

LORD,
You said you'll never leave me,
Never forsake me.
You'll test my spirit,
You won't allow it to break me,
You'll carry my weight until the end.

LORD,
You're my *Savior*!
My *Maker*!
My *Friend*!

I can always count on you!

I Wished You Were There

From the very first day I spoke my first word,
    I wished you were there.
From the very first day I took my first step,
    I wished you were there.
From the very first day I lost my first tooth,
    I wished you were there.
From the very first day I rode my first bike,
    I wished you were there.
From the very first day I read my first book,
    I wished you were there.
From the very first day I started my first day of school,
    I wished you were there.
From the very first day I'd gotten my first "A",
    I wished you were there.
From the very first day I went on my first date,
    I wished you were there.
From the very first day I went to the prom,
    I wished you were there.
From the very first day I graduated high school,
    I wished you were there.
From the very first day I decided to join the Navy,
    I wished you were there.
From the very first day I graduated college,
    I wished you were there.
From the very first day I became a Navy officer,
    I wished you were there.
From the very first day I walked down the aisle,
    I wished you were there.
Throughout my life when I needed you the most,
    I wished you were there.
In your absence, *My Mother* was always there,
    To comfort me, to hold me and to guide me.
Even though, I wished you were there!

Innocence

Youthful,
Vibrant,
Caring
And Free.

Untamed,
Untouched,
Unsoiled,
Purity.

Not yet tempted
By the sins of the world,
Remaining true to your character.
The innocence of a little boy or girl.

Look at Me Now

Look at me now,
I'm on top of the world.
I've come along way
From a scared little girl.

I never gave up,
I knew I could make it.
I followed my dreams,
I was determined to make it.

I can't believe I'm here,
Look at where I've been.
It's been a long journey,
One I thought would never end.

I fought hard along the way,
Had the door slammed in my face.
Was it because I'm a girl?
Was it because of my race?

I never gave up,
I was determined to make it.
With the glass ceiling over my head,
I was determined to break it.

I shattered the glass,
I broke down the walls;
Finally making it to the top,
Standing strong, standing tall!
Look at me now.

Looks are Deceiving

You possess a smile that is bright
from a life filled with love, laughter and joy.
When looked upon by many faces
your spirit is felt, its ready to deploy.

You gracefully touch the hearts of others
by comforting them in times of pain.
You fill their lives with love and happiness
in hopes to never experience hurt again.

You have the ability to move mountains,
you possess tenacity, determination and drive.
You can lead an army into battle,
having faith in you to survive.

You have the courage of a lion,
the strength of a thousand bears.
You will give of your heart with compassion
while protecting the boundary of your lair.

One should never be fooled
by the youthful look upon your face.
However charmed by your innocent smile,
one should never cross you or step out of place.

Ole' Tyme Keepa

Is it real?
This feeling I feel
Deep within my soul,
Tellin me 'I'm gettin old.

Tyme is tickin,
Tick tock – Tick tock
Goes the clock.
Ole' Tyme Keepa' of my age,
My mind, my body and my soul.

I'm weary 'bout how I feel,
Can't stop that clock that goes
Tick tock – Tick tock,
Ol' Tyme Keepa' of my age,
My mind, my body and my soul.

STOP!
Let me rewind,
Go back in time,
I can't grow old,
I haven't lived yet.
Wanna' bet?!

My hair ain't grey.
My skin ain't wrinkled or dry.
I'm too young to say good-bye.
Good-bye to life?

I'm a wife to my husband.
I'm a mother to my child.
I still wanna' live a while.

So I gotta' stop that clock that goes
Tick tock - Tick tock,
Ole' Tyme Keepa' of my age,
My mind, my body and my soul.

Our Black is Beautiful

Our black is beautiful,
more beautiful than the
most precious *Black Rose*.

Our black is beautiful,
despite the false stories
we've been told.

Our black is *so* beautiful,
just look in the mirror
tell me what you see?

An African King?
A Prince?
A Princess?
Maybe an African Queen?

Yes!
You're black is beautiful,
despite the false stories
you've been told.

After years of being denied
access to our history;
tales of how *our* ancestors
were kidnapped, bought and sold.

Tales of how *our* ancestors
were bred like cattle.

Tales of how *our* ancestors
were whipped, hung or killed
if they should ever gather together to battle.

Battle *slave masters* who'd gotten rich
off *our* ancestors' blood,
sweat and tears.

Who for centuries,
violated *our* ancestors human rights
while instilling in their minds fear.

Who for centuries,
oppressed the minds
of the next generations to come.

Who for centuries,
hung and killed black men,
and brutally *raped* black women.

Yet despite all that...
Our black is beautiful!
Just look in the mirror,
tell me what you see?

A Warrior!
A King!
A Queen!
Throne rulers of our destiny.

My black is beautiful!
Despite what they say.
Your black is beautiful!
Our black is beautiful!

Remind yourself of this fact, each and every day.

Our Legacy

Throughout our history,
Black woman have always contributed
to the advancement of the *Black* race.
These modern day *S'heros*, famous *Pioneers*,
have left behind honorary legacies
that we should all embrace.

From the likes of,
The legacy of *Queen of Sheba*,
she sought the wisdom of King Solomon,
for whom she bore his son.
Into the 21st[th] century
their royal African linage has been past-down.

The legacy of *Sojourner Truth*,
whose perseverance we'll never forget.
Her unyielding strength and implacable passion,
defined her zealous character
and her amazing intellect.
As a black woman, she demanded respect
in her notable speech, *"Ain't I woman?!"*
in such a time, in *Black American* history
when lynching blacks folks was on the rise.

The legacy of *Harriet Tubman*,
she was known as the '*Moses*' of her times.
She gave of her life
on a quest for humanitarian rights,
a candle light for her vibrant spirit
still shines.

The legacy of *Phillis Wheately*,
who is honored for being the first black
published poet and writer.
Her magnificent poems
avowed her independence,
she was an *emancipated* freedom fighter.

Her remarkable works of poetry
gave birth to more famous black poets
and writers to come.
Her eloquent poems brought her fame
during the *American Revolution.*
She was highly respected and admired
amongst such political figures as, *George Washington.*

The legacy of *Mary McLeod Bethune,*
co-founder of Bethune-Cookman
historical black college.
She was a civil rights leader, philosopher,
educator and prominent political advisor.
Her legacy speaks truth of our struggles
and remarkable survival.

The legacy of *Dr. Maya Angelou,*
prestigiously honored poet,
civil rights activist,
first black woman director and writer.
Her famous poems:
"Phenomenal Woman and *Still I Rise"*
continues to inspire black women
to reach for the prize!

The legacy of *Nikki Giovanni,*
world-renowned poet, writer, commentator,
civil rights activist, author and educator.
Her famous poem: *"Cotton Candy on a Rainy"*
(highly admired by my mother)
speaks of a woman's trivial issues,
difficulties and blues,
from her absolute mundane- gray days.

The most recent and *honorable* addition
to this narrative list of legacies,
sits at the side of America's first black President,
Michelle Obama, America's First Lady.
Since her reign, Michelle has graced us all
with her poise and amazing intellect.

Her compassion for
wanting to help others,
her voice to our country,
signifies that she is truly blessed.

Whether born of royal African linage,
a slave or born free,
each of these magnificent women
leaves behind a remarkable legacy.

Depicted by tales of their joy,
victory, pain and sorrow,
each of their legacies will continue to define us
as, *"Beautiful Black Women"*
yesterday, today and tomorrow.

As they pass us the torch,
Black women, let's receive it and continue to reign.
Let us proudly leave behind *our* legacies,
passing down *our* heritage
to *our* beautiful *black* children.

Sistahs,
We are Black Queens, Black Goddesses,
we possess remarkable strength.
Exhibited by *our* character, *our* tenacity,
our ability to stand strong (*oftentimes alone*),
on our own two feet.

Sistahs,
You are the *Rock*!
You're the *Foundation,*
there is no one else like you.
So continue to carry the torch
as beautiful *Black Queens,*
by always excelling in everything you do!

Pain

Pain is what I felt
when I was belittled to nothing less,
causing grief and anxiety,
feelings of hopelessness.

When I was forced to submit to
verbal, physical, unremitting sexual abuse,
being used and disposed of is inhumane.
There's no excuse!

Escaping from this demon,
on the run to try and hide;
seeking to escape the insecurities
of what I feel inside.

Left emotionally and physically
scarred from the pain.
Years of living in hell, purgatory.
LORD, please help me,
release me from these chains!

Pain in Our Lives

With each passing day of our lives,
when we suffer a tragedy,
we will try to go on living
like there's nothing wrong;
never facing reality.

By ignoring the *pain in our lives,*
we hope that someday
the pain will be set free.

Be it the loss of a loved one;
a sister, a mother, a brother, a son,
a daughter, a father or a friend.

It's hard to let go of the pain
and suffering from a tragedy.
It's even harder to accept the reality
of *the pain in our lives.*

But we must try to go on living,
by hoping and praying that someday
the pain will be set free.

Perseverance

When faced with adversity
    I will stand my ground,
Even if I shall falter
    Or if my judgment is not sound,
I will stand firm on my conviction
    By always serving the LORD,
My feet will remain on solid ground,
    I will never get discouraged.
Once… Twice…
    I will rebound!

Power of Hope

To dream beyond measure,
To not accept defeat,
No ladder is too high to climb,
No mountain is to steep.

Hope is fortitude,
It's the center of one's core,
One's covenant with GOD,
His ability to open doors.

Life is not eternal,
It could be over in the blink of an eye,
So always pursue your dreams,
Your promise to GOD,
Your destiny,
Before you die.

Prayer of Hope

Dear LORD,
I come to you on my knees *in prayer,*
to ask you to strengthen my spirit.

My soul has been weakened
from years of much despair.
My lonely heart is broken,
in dire need of *your* repair.

My soul is captured in anguish,
filled with enduring pain.
My spirit is quickly fading,
I want to go on living.

LORD,
I need your courage and wisdom
to go on living a little longer,
please bless me with your mighty strength,
allowing my spirit to be stronger.

Protectors of Freedom

Some say war is not the answer
to bring about peace,
when fighting for what we believe in,
whether for religious or other beliefs.

We are all *Protectors of Freedom,*
commissioned by GOD
to bring *Peace* and *Unity*
throughout the world.

Fighting to protect the liberties
of our families, the *unalienable rights*
of every young boy and girl.

We are all *Guardians* of human life,
protectors of our Great *Nation;*
defenders of human rights
and all of GOD's creations.

Rescue Yourself

Free yourself from a life of hell,
whether from a bad relationship
with an abusive spouse
or prison cell.

Release yourself from physical
or mental abuse.
To remain a victim of such treatment
is a piteous excuse.

Trying to conceal the agony
of what you feel inside;
the scars on your face,
you can no longer hide.

The thought of walking away
feels worse than living in hell,
not knowing what tomorrow may bring,
the misery is far too much to dwell.

Rescue yourself from this life of pain,
there's always hope.
It's time to break free
and live your life again!

Respect

When you belittle me,
Berate me,
Oftentimes negate me;
Should I respect you?

When you dishonor me,
Abuse me,
Oftentimes refuse me;
Should I respect you?

When you ignore me,
Judge me,
Oftentimes begrudge me;
Should I respect you?

One should never
Belittle,
Berate
Or negate.

Dishonor,
Abuse
Or refuse.

Ignore,
Misjudge
Or begrudge;
'Cause no one's perfect!

Live your life
By setting positive examples,
And always show others
Respect!

Self – Reflection

Staring back at me
at times with a twinkle in my eye.
Able to reveal what I'm thinking,
whether it's the truth or a lie.

Able to detect the joy
or sadness that I feel.
Looking beyond a painted illusion,
exposing what is real.

A lonely spirit whose soul is lost
becomes vulnerable to human needs.
Man's desire to feed upon the flesh
by destroying faith and planting seeds.

You can't hide from what you see before you;
a painted illusion, an art of perfection.
The eyes are a pathway to your soul
and so is the mirror of 'Self – Reflection.'

Shades of Blackness

I see the rays of light shine through,
Casting down on something new,
As beautiful, as beautiful as you.

The many rays of light,
Some dark, some shadowed,
Some bright.

Reflecting on different shades
Of our past, the hidden secrets
Sprouted from splendid grass.

Our Roots,
The different *Shades of Blackness*,
Is our history that's been buried with the rest.

We must revive the past
And learn from our mistakes,
Because *our* history, *our* future,
Is *ours*, not theirs to take.

She's My Hero
(Dedicated to the memory of Major, Gloria Davis)

Sitting here numb, in search of the right words to say,
I get down on my knees in prayer, asking the LORD,
"Why have you taken my best-friend away?"

Softly he whispers,
"My child, it's because I needed her this day."

She blessed so many lives with her caring ways,
She charmed so many hearts with her glowing smile,
She warmed so many souls with her humble spirit,
She was simply adored for her alluring style.

Now it's time for her to be amongst the heavenly angels,
Where she will continue to watch over
The countless lives she's touched.

The emptiness and loneliness in your heart
Is a constant reminder
That she is missed very much!

Remember my child,
"Always be kind and gentle to everyone you meet,
Show compassion, love and respect for others,
Even someone you casually meet in the street."

By believing in yourself,
Others will always believe in you.
By respecting yourself,
Others will always respect you.

Live your life unselfishly
And remain true to who you *really* are.
Just like your best-friend Gloria,
One day you too will become
A bright- shining *Star*.

Silence

Awake meditation.
My soul becoming one with my spirit,
Inspiration.

Me loving me and nothing else.
My alone time with GOD,
Conversations with myself.

It's when I self-reflect,
When I hear truth.
It's when GOD guides my spirit
On what to do.

It's when I feel more alive,
When I can see the heavens beyond the clouds.
When my spirit is set free.

It's when I know I'm not alone,
It's when GOD speaks to me.

Smile

When I thought of you today,
    my heart smiled.
The familiar smile
    when you make me laugh.
The familiar smile
    when you make me cry.
The familiar smile
    when I say, "Thank you"
For putting a smile on my face.

Solitude

Listening to the smooth sounds
of soothing jazz,
walking on white sand beaches
hand in hand.

Taking a peaceful stroll in the park,
enjoying a quiet evening alone
by candlelight or in the dark.

Solitude is a quiet place,
a place to relax and clear you mind,
away from all the chaos in the world
or other distractions of mankind.

Solitude is your inner peace,
a place to cleanse your soul.
Solitude is a place of spiritual isolation,
a place of rejuvenation;
without fear of growing old.

Sorrow

The suffering I feel
in the absence of your love,
although you're no longer here
you're all I ever think of.

My days are filled with sadness
from the madness of this world,
as expressed upon the many faces
of a lost little boy or girl.

With each passing day
you are truly missed,
within my heart and soul
is where our treasured memories
will always exist.

Still is the Moment in Time

Abandoned like a wandering child,
no one there to hear his cry;
isolated from the rest of the world.

Pain is the darkness revealed
from a single look into the eye
of an abandoned boy or girl.

Still is the moment in time
when there's no motion,
no feelings; life passes us by.

To care and show emotion
for their suffering,
it'll break your heart
and make you cry.

To watch the sadness in their eyes
your heart aches from the madness
of the rest of the world;
in all the confusion from the illusion
that the world really cares.

Do you ignore the cry from their pain
or the aching in their heart?
They're all alone in the cold,
left abandoned in the dark.

Rescue a lonely child, give them hope
that they can change the world,
from all the confusion and false illusions
to show that the *World* really cares.

Successful

Is what you strive to become.
When you reach the top
You become number one.

You're at the top,
You've accomplished all of your goals.
You've become something new,
You were tired of the old.

Keep in mind,
Always strive to succeed.
Keep up your pride
And do all good deeds.

You will look back on your life
And see a remarkable change.
All in all, *Success* is what you will gain.

Talk to Me

My child,
You look discouraged,
Tell me what's on your mind,
Talk to me...

Let me hear your voice,
Tell me what's wrong,
Let me hear your cry,
Talk to me...

From the heavens above
I look down upon your face,
I can see your pain,
Talk to me...

My child,
Let me answer your prayers,
To ease away your pain,
Talk to me...

Take Back Our Children

How do we take back our children?
I ask myself this question
each time I see a news story about,
"A young black boy or girl getting shot."

How do we take back our children?
I ask myself this question
each time I hear a young black mother
tellin' her daughter, who's less than five years old,
"Go head 'baby gurl', that's right, do it like ya' moma
and "*Drop it like it's hot*!"

How do we take back our children?
I ask myself this question,
each time I hear a rap song about:
"Twerkin', rainin'- droppin' dollars,
clockin' or pimpin' hoes."

How do we take back our children?
I ask myself this question,
each time I hear a young black woman talking about,
"Gettin' her hair and nails done" before goin' clubin',
to look for a new man to buy her some mo'
"tight-fittin' clothes."

How do we take back our children?
I ask myself this question
each time I hear of a new statistic
on the news or the Internet about:
"Police brutality or "*Black on Black*" crime."

How do we take back our children?
I ask myself this question
each time I hear of a new statistic about
"How young black children
are growing up without their parents;
being raised by other family members
or forced to live in foster homes,

or in the streets; 'cause their mom or dad is dead,
addicted to drugs or in prison - doin' time."

How do we take back our children?
We take back our children by
"Taking back our communities!"

Teardrops

I watch the tear drops
 fall from your saddened eyes.
Your heart is stricken by grief
 over a loved one who recently died.
If I could alleviate your pain
 I would surely try.
In the meantime,
 allow me to wipe away the *teardrops*
from your weeping eyes.

The Demon Within

It has been released,
the demon from within.
It has no name or origin,
it has no kin.

It exposes its ugly face
by attacking from all sides,
after reaping so much havoc
it leaves and tries to hide.

Who is this fearful demon,
this evil spirit with no name?
Creating so much chaos,
inflicting so much pain?

Leaving me to question
if my love for you is real?
The many faces of this demon
is amazingly surreal.

This emotion that I feel for you
is as real as it was before;
stretching from every mountaintop,
beyond the ivory shores.

Let's keep this demon buried
so far deep underground,
in the pit of cold and darkness
where it's empty with no sound.

Let's rid our hearts of this demon
to fill with love and laughter,
let's cleanse our souls of insecurities
and live happily ever after.

The Great Sentinel

Hear ye!
Hear ye!
Hear ye!

The time has come
to call upon my mighty warriors:
"The Protectors of our Freedom,
The Guardians of Peace,
And the heroic *Dark Knights."*

As your mighty appointed General, *"The Great Sentinel"*
I summon you to carry out the LORD's will,
"Defend this sacred land. Preserve the human race
and all of humanity."

Cast out the devil and his evil ways,
Protect human souls into the after-life,
And continue to carry out the LORD's will.

The Persistence of Memory

A time piece, washed upon the shores.
Remnants of your memories
lies within each layer of my core.

Traveling through life
as tiny pieces of *Father Time*,
eventually I will fade away;

Returning back to the sea,
then back to earth;
our memories- intertwined.

The Sound of Music

Harmony, beats and rhythm,
a composition of melodic sounds;
composed in different genres
for the purpose of *getting down.*

Whether for easy listening,
Classical, Jazz, Pop, Reggae, R & B
or Rock and Roll;

Music is delightful, it's satisfying,
it soothes your inner spirit
and pleases your inner soul.

To Be Black Like Me

To be black like me,
is to always lift your head high.
To be black like me,
is to tell the world why!

Why am I treated different?!
Is it because of the color of my skin?
When color shouldn't matter,
it's the content of one's character,
what they possess within.

Yet *da' man* will attempt to judge you
for whom he thinks you are;
falsely labeling you as: "A dead-beat,
someone on welfare, a thug,
or maybe a *Rap Star.*"

Better yet, "An angry black woman"
or "A black man who should be
locked up behind bars."
Being black means,
"You will always have to go through life
having to defend who you truly are."

Whether you are rich or poor,
educated with multiple college degrees,
"If you are not black,
you'll never know what it's like
to live on this earth, in my world,
being *Black* like me!

Tormented Heart

Desolate from the rest of the world,
a lost soul- lonely and extremely shy.
Weightless, like a drifting feather,
free to roam and soar the open sky.

Empty, like the pit of a well
when there's no rain,
my soul is hollow;
once filled with love
now lies completely dry.

Pain, is the torment in my heart
revealed from a single glance
when you look into my dying eyes.

Still, is the moment in time
when there's no motion;
our tender lives passes us by.

Breathless, to inhale and breathe again,
I ask myself, "To go on living my life
without you, should I try?"

Numb, when there's no more pain,
agony or emotion; my body lifeless
when I die.

True Faces

We awaken to live out our fantasies,
our daily lives compound.
Faces change, different cities,
many lights, different sounds.

We seek fact from fiction,
on a quest to know what's real.
As we travel and meet new people,
we don't know who's fake
or who's for-real.

We want to get to know them
to share thoughts of who we are.
We are many miles away from home,
the journey seemed so far.

Our parents taught us good values,
taught us right from wrong.
Yet they didn't prepare us for what to do
when things go wrong.

Influenced by those around us
we begin to act confused;
caught up in a whirlwind,
we don't know what to do.

We begin to ask questions,
"If all that's around us is real?"
Voices are strange,
lights are different
and the faces seem surreal.

As we continue to go through life
we must remember all that's changed;
the different cities, many lights,
and the faces with no name.

To separate fact from fiction
you should always seek the truth,
always be honest with yourself
and others will be honest with you.

You are My Rock

You are my rock,
My spiritual inspiration,
To my life you bring joy and celebration,
You are my rock!

It's hard to find a friend,
Someone who is loving and kind.
It's hard to find a friend
Who's there for you all the time.

It's hard to find a friend
Who'll accept you for who you are.
It's hard to find a friend
To call on and will be there.

Your friendship means the world to me,
When times are bad you're by my side.
You'll give me a shoulder to lean on,
A listening ear you'll provide.

When I'm confused
You'll give advice to me,
You're a mentor and a friend.
You'll never pass judgment,
You're by my side til' the end.

I can tell you my secrets,
I can *never* tell you a lie.
You'll always keep me honest,
In you, I can always confide.

I can count on you
Forever til' the end,
There's no better blessing
Than to have you as a friend,
You are my rock!

You are Somebody

Don't turn your back on someone
who's crying out for love.
We should embrace all GOD's children
by giving them a hug.

Tell him or her, "*You are somebody!*"
Not to waste their lives in the street.
Teach them to open up their hearts to GOD,
yet be weary of those they meet.

We are all vulnerable to those
who make *false promises* by telling lies.
Those who worship *false idols*
won't go to heaven when they die.

This world we live in is plagued with
sex, drugs, lies, *false idols*
and deadly diseases.

Turn your life over to GOD,
who will never forsake you.
'Cause *GOD* creates miracles
for both you and me.

You Give Me Strength

You woke me this morning,
helping me to get out of bed.
I dreamt of so many things last night,
the thoughts are still circling inside my head.

Telling me,
"I have the strength and the courage
to do what I have to do."
Owing all the praise and glory
to no one other than *You.*

LORD, you give me strength,
you make me whole.
You give me guidance,
through you I am bold;

Bold enough to take on any challenge
that's before me every day.
Whenever I am weak or weary,
I get down on my knees and pray.

You pick me up,
I stand tall.
I'm strong enough
to battle it all!

'Cause LORD,
You are my strength!
You make me whole!
You give me guidance,
through you "I Am Bold!"

Bold enough to take on any challenge
that's before me every day.

Love, Hope and Happiness

A Life Time of Love

A life time of love begins now,
to determine the right time for love
I ask, "How?"

Neither a date, nor a timeline
can dictate when true love begins.
True love is eternal, lasting a lifetime,
it's to infinity; it never ends.

True love is determined by destiny,
one's original life's design.
Predetermined by fate;
two hearts intertwined.

No matter how many times
you try to test your original life's design,
you'll experience many trials and tribulations;
only to lose every time.

True love is not a *guessing* game
to determine who'll win or lose,
by attempting to change your destiny
for whomever *you* want to choose.

Failing to understand how it works,
you'll fall short every time.
Like the forces of nature's fury,
one can never change *your* original life's design.

Only the LORD knows
the most compatible soul mates,
it's not a guessing game
left for you and I to debate.

So let nature run its course
to bring two souls together as one,
to share in *"A Life Time of Love,"*
and enjoy a happy and blissful union.

Black Rose

Soft
Honest
Gentle
Delicate
Pure

Fragrant
Special
Pleasing
Satisfying

Full blossom
Radiant
Exotic
Beautiful

Stunning
Elegant
Exciting
Seductive

Exotic
Tranquil
Erotic
Ecstasy

Thankful
Graceful
Compassionate
Inspiration

Rejuvenation
Celebration
Liberation
Eternal
Life

Broken Heart

We once shared our lives together,
we were more than just friends.
You asked for my hand in marriage,
vowing to always love me 'til the end.'

Our lives are different now,
we have drifted apart.
You've moved on with someone else,
leaving me with a *broken heart*.

My heart would never know
why our relationship had to end this way.
The love in my heart, reserved just for you,
is eternal; it will never fade away.

By My Side, I Need You Here

The tears of my heart are calling you,
crying out to release the pain.
Torn from years of loving you,
I swore I could never love again.

Caught up in the mist of reality,
my mind is so confused.
Don't know if I'm coming or going,
without you what's a girl to do?

Baby I need you,
I breathe you,
without you there's no air.

I gotta' have you,
I wanna' hold you,
'By my side, I need you here.'

My heart is on the verge of exploding,
like a rocket launched into space;
set out on a course to the oblivion,
for your love I will not chase.

My life has room for only you,
I can't bear no more pain;
I am willing to break my promise
and fall in love with you again.

Baby, I need you,
I breathe you,
without you there's no air.

I gotta' to have you,
I wanna' to hold you,
'By my side, I need you here'.

Cancer

The calling of the sea
    beckons me;
Inviting me to feel her wetness,
    Her depth.
Her full bodied waves of temptations,
    Her roaring mist,
Her calmness,
    Her thundering rain.
Her beauty,
    Her glow,
Her distance,
    Her peace.
Inviting me home

Casey

(Dedicated to my mother)

Caring soul, loving heart and child of God
Always doing acts of good-will for others
Special, I am to God, in every single way
Easy going and vibrant, always full of hope
Youthful is how I feel, each and every day

Chaotic Love

What is this,
that has my mind going crazy;
completely out of control.

What is this,
that has such a grasp on my heart,
I can't escape the capture of its strong hold.

Seeking to find the answer,
I search deep within.
My emotions embodied in chaos
sends my mind into a tail-spin.

Searching for the answer,
I look up to the stars above.
As GOD touches my kindled spirit,
He says, "My child, it's only Love."

Cherished Love

(Inspired by artist Thomas Blackshear's figurine — Cherished)

I see you knelt before me,
I offer you my warm embrace;
Secured within my bosom,
Your head I gently place.

We speak no words,
We hear no sounds;
We both know
This familiar place;

It harbors the love we share,
The love we will forever cherish.
As I stand here,
You knelt before me, humbled,
Our infinite love will never perish.

Dark Knight

(Inspired by artist Thomas Blackshear's figurine – Dark Knight)

Tall, dark and handsome,
an intriguing specimen you are.
Has the LORD answered my prayers
from wishing upon a star?

Sending me my *Black Prince*,
my *Dark Knight* in shining armor.
Someone who'll fulfill my longing desire,
waiting in anticipation, my curiosity wonders.

Will you satisfy my existence with happiness,
provide security and fill the emptiness in my life?
Will you complete me, by making me whole,
will I ultimately become your wife?

Yes! My prayers have been answered
by the LORD Almighty from above;
to you, my *Black Prince*, I offer a description
of what my heart defines as, *'True Love'* ...

Some may call you my *Support*,
I will call you my *Dark Knight*.

Some may call you my *Better Half*,
I will call you my *Dark Knight*.

Some may call you my *Rock*,
I will call you my *Dark Knight*.

He, who rescued me from the pain,
once deep rooted in my heart;
tearing into my soul, ripping it apart.

Who bravely rescued me from my past,
from bad relationships that didn't last;
ultimately rescuing me from myself,
by delivering me into the light.

My heart belongs to you,
"My true love, my Black Prince;
my honorary *Dark Knight*.

Dedication of Love

I dedicate this poem to the man I love,
My heavenly Prince
Sent from the heavens above.

You keep me honest and faithful,
You are truly my man.
You give me purpose for living,
You accept me for who I am.

With you, I'm not afraid
To share pain from my past.
It's shown me heartache,
It's taught me how to believe in true love,
Our love, that will forever last.

With you, I'm whole,
My life feels complete.
I'm not afraid to take a chance at *love*,
I will not accept defeat.

We are not just two souls
Passing in the night,
I'm fully committed to only you
And I vow to treat you right.

Emancipated Love

When they look at us,
They will stare;
Their eyes will reveal their thoughts.
What are they thinking?
Should we care?

As we walk hand in hand,
Kiss and embrace;
Two souls will ignite
A mystifying spirit,
Releasing a halo of love.

Fueled by passion,
Fueled by pain,
Fueled by hate.
Fueled by time, lost.

Emancipated love,
Familiar and welcomed.
Old love set free.

Liberated souls,
A modern day love affair, *Soul mates*.
It's who we are meant to be.

Energizing Love

You keep my spirit alive
from an external port.
Connected to my heart,
you're my life support.

You energize my soul
when I'm feeling your vibe,
like the rhythmic movement of a dancer,
so energetic, so alive!

Your vibe sends pulses through my veins
by stimulating my heart,
igniting my internal flame
with but one single spark.

This spark of your love potion
has me going through the motions,
causing me to lose complete control.
My mind is going crazy
from the absence of your love
which has taken its toll.

While searching for the answer
as to why you're not here,
my pulse fades quickly
'cause your spirit's not near.

Leaving me feeling *motionless*,
lifeless, my body is numb;
without the strength of your love
my life will succumb.

I need the ability to survive
independent on my own,
so I won't stop living
whenever I'm alone.

Your vibe inspires the strength
I possess deep within my soul,
removing the insecurities
of being alone and growing old.

If I disconnect your chord
will my love for you die?
Can I survive on my own,
when I'm left to be alone?
Do I have to, should I try?

Will I still love and respect you,
when I'm forced to live without you?
Will I be submissive and supportive
in all that I do?

Only you can provide the answers
to the questions above. For now,
I need you to reenergize my spirit
with the joy of your love.

First Love

Familiar, yet distant.
Shared emotions
From a lifetime ago.

Harbored feelings,
Never lost, buried deep;
Never let go.

First love,
Lost love,
Only love;
Feelings bestowed.

Pain,
Ache,
Hurt,
Sorrow.

Sad,
Joy,
Confused,
Angry!

Hushed,
Secrecy,
Shame,
Kept!

These are the feelings I felt
When I looked into your welcoming eyes.
When I heard the sound of your masculine,
Familiar voice, my heart began to melt.

Twenty years later…
Do I, do we,
Now have a choice?
I chose love. Do you?

Fortress of Love

Can I tear down this fortress
which protects my heart and my soul?
By allowing you back into my life,
will you make my life complete?
Will I be made whole?

Can you take away the pain I felt
when you left me all alone?
Can you payback the time I lost
from the countless nights I spent alone?

At this point, what can you do?
What can you say?
For you to walk back into my life
won't take the pain in my heart away.

You stand before me
to plea for my forgiveness.
Should I accept the offering of your love,
or should I resist?
Does the flame that once ignited our passion
still exist?

My heart, still protected says, "No!"
My mind over matter says,
"Take it slow!"

Have You Ever Said, Yes

Have you ever said, Yes?
Yes, to a million things.
Yes, to a million ways,
To show how much you care?

Have you ever said, Yes?
Yes, to I do.
Yes, to I love you,
When asked will you be mine?

Have you ever said, Yes?
Yes, to I will never leave you.
Yes, to I will always support you,
To show how much you care?

Have you ever said, Yes?
Yes, to you will never falter.
Yes, while standing at the altar
When asked, "Will you be mine?"

Have you ever said, Yes?...

I Wanna Be With You

Hey baby stop for a minute,
it's been several years
since we've been making out,
so I guess I'm your *fella?*

We started out as friends,
friends with benefits,
no strings attached,
no commitment;
back then I was ok with that.

Many years have gone by.
Baby I know I'm ready,
to be your man, your lover,
your one and only steady.

I wanna' be with you,
    for more than just one night.
I wanna' be with you,
    we deserve to be together.
I wanna' be with you,
    for more than just one night.
I wanna' be with you,
    no more part-time lovers.

We've been denying each other
'cause of issues from the past;
afraid of true love, a commitment,
out of fear that our love won't last.

We need to put the past behind us
and commit to what we want,
that's each-other.

No more friends with benefits.
I wanna' be the one,
your one and only lover!

My feelings for you have changed
and I'm ready to devote to you, my life.
I want a true commitment,
to be honest and faithful;
girl I want you as my wife.

I wanna' be with you,
        for more than just one night.
I wanna' be with you,
        we deserve to be together.
I wanna' be with you,
        for more than just one night.
I wanna' be with you,
        no more part-time lovers.

If

If...   There was no more sunshine,
If...   There was no more rain,
If...   I would have forgiven you,
Would I be left to suffer heartache and pain?

If...   There were no more rainbows,
If...   There was no heaven above,
If...   I would have forgiven you,
Would my heart be filled with love?

If...   There was always sunshine,
If...   There was always rain,
If...   There were always rainbows and heaven,
If...   I were to forgive you,
In my heart, my love for you, I would bestow!

Incarceration of Love

There's no need to say good-bye,
my love for you will never die.
No amount of distance
can separate our hearts,
our love is bond, even when
we're physically apart.

The image of your handsome face
is one I can never erase.
The years of memories we've shared,
to wait for me will show you care.

The last words you said to me,
"I Love you,"
are cherished in my mind.
Yet my heart needs to know
if you will save your love for me
while I'm doing *hard-time*?"

My heart aches for only you
and I know that you hate it,
that you're not able
to hold me in your arms
because I'm *incarcerated*.

Inside of Me

I saw a picture of you today;
It startled me,
It excited me,
It motivated me.

It inspired me,
It moved me,
It humbled me.

It awakened me,
It saddened me,
It reminded me…

I smiled,
The smile you always bring out of me
Because you are forever
Inside of me.

Is it Possible

What is this thing called love?
Could it be the love we once shared is pure?
As innocent as the first day we met,
when your eyes gazed into my soul.
When my ears first heard the polite sound
of your adolescent voice.

We were younger than most teenagers
who shared the same notion of *puppy love*.
Ours was different, it was forbidden,
as forbidden as the *forbidden* fruit
in the *Garden of Eden*.

Down *South*, over twenty years ago,
there were certain things folks back then
didn't openly talk about.
Like the forbidden love shared between
black and white folks.

This was during the time
when white folks in the South,
tried to *teach* black folks *"their place"*
in their white *Southern* society.

Our love never had such boundaries.
When we shared our first kiss
it was as natural as the summer rain.

It was welcomed,
It was desired,
It was intoxicating,
It was blissful.

Some folks say, "History has a strange way
of repeating itself." I must agree.
When I watch the local Atlanta news,
there's just as much blatant talk of racism- today,
than over twenty years ago.

Despite *Southern* society prejudices,
my heart still yearns and desires
our innocent adolescent love.

When I heard your voice again,
after all those years,
I could feel the butterflies in my stomach
doing a victory dance, singing and rejoicing
to our rekindled *puppy love.*
What did they know that I didn't know?

This is my mind and my body,
yet I can't control this feeling inside me.
A feeling I haven't felt in a long time,
the same feeling I felt when I experienced
my first school girl crush.

A feeling I've anticipated
for several decades,
reuniting me with my childhood *love.*

Is it possible,
to love you again after all these years?
Is it possible,
I never fell out of love with you?
Is it possible,
that a white man can openly love
a black woman in the South?
Or a *black woman* can openly love
a *white man* in the South,
without fear of racial prejudice?
Is it possible?

It's the End of a Love Affair

It's the end of a love affair,
But my mind can't go nowhere.

I'm always thinking about you;
Your pretty brown eyes,
Your lovely dark skin,
The smell of your hair,
The places we've been.

It's the end of a love affair,
But my mind can't go nowhere.

I'm always thinking about you
With everything I do,
But my heart can't move on.
I tell myself each and every day,
"I gotta move on"
But my mind is here to stay.

If I put these words in a song
I'll call it, *"It's the end of a love affair"*
But my mind can't go nowhere.

When we were together,
You said you will love me forever
But you have moved on,
I have try to do the same.
When I make love to someone else
I wanna scream out *your* name.

Our love didn't last,
I gotta put my thoughts in the past,
'Cause *it's the end of a love affair,*
But my mind can't go nowhere.

Journey of Love

On your journey
to find true love,
you'll experience
many trials and tribulations.

You must heal
your wounded heart,
before reaching
your final destination.

Put your past behind you
and prepare your life
for something new.

Be fully committed,
honest and faithful,
and believe your love is true.

Leap of Fate

Majestic mountains,
peaks so high;
deep blue seas,
sails pass us by.

Taking a leap of fate
into the open sky;
beneath our feet
nothing lies.

Floating through the air,
our spirits are set free;
feeling so alive
knowing always and forever
we'll be.

Fear not the unknown
on our journey to find true love,
no longer will we wait.

Like *heavenly angels,*
free to roam the open sky,
our souls shall forever mate.

A symphony of love
is the beautiful music
our spirits will create.

Letting Go of the Pain

I spent many years in agony,
each day I prayed
for the pain in my heart
to go away.

Years began to multiply,
months grew longer,
time became endless days.

I had to get away
and leave the only life I knew behind.
I needed to gather my composure,
come to my senses,
before losing control of my mind.

While rebuilding my new life,
I'd enriched my spirit and cleansed my soul.
By regaining my independence,
I became whole.

Assessing my new found life,
my spirit was enlightened,
I had prepared myself for someone new.

My prayers had been answered
by our *Heavenly Father,*
God blessed my new life with *You*!

A proud man, with a kind and gentle heart,
possessing all I'll ever need.
You helped to ease away my pain
by inspiring my soul;
I submit to you to take the lead.

To lead me on a journey of new love,
taking paths never traveled,
filled with passion and pure bliss.

The life I knew before,
once filled with sadness and pain,
is a life I'll never miss.

My days are brighter now,
you've brought me happiness,
love, inspiration and joy.

Having you in my life,
always by my side,
each day is a new day
to be thankful to GOD,
and to always cherish and enjoy.

Life Without You

When I look into your pretty brown eyes,
you bring rejuvenation back into my life.
Since the very first day I met you,
I knew that you would later become my wife.

I was always running from a commitment,
afraid that I would never find true love.
Having you in my life makes my life complete,
you're all I'll ever need or ever dream of.

Together we have chemistry,
without you my life has no meaning,
no purpose at all.

To go on living in this world, without you,
I would rather not go on living
without you, or at all!

Lonely Heart

Each day I hope and pray
that my feelings for you won't fade away.
My emotions seems so out of place,
like something is missing from my heart,
it's just an empty space.

This void in my heart is reserved just for you,
without you here by my side, what's a girl to do?
Fill it with someone new, just to take up space?
Because you're not here, should you be replaced?

I don't know how much longer
I can take being alone;
without you here by my side
this house is just an empty home.

Please answer the call of my broken heart,
calling out to you to mend the *part*
that separates our lonely souls.
Let's mend the gap between us
so *two* souls can become *one*,
making *us* whole.

Love Is

The twitch you get in your heart
that tells you how you feel.
The twinkle that shines in your eyes
that expresses what you feel, 'is real!'

An unconditional emotion
aroused from deep inside,
an expression of openness
when there's nothing to hide.

Love is a truism,
the realism of sensations
that comes straight from the heart.
Conveyed by your actions, your words,
or even through creative '*works of art*'.

Love can be displayed
in different forms or fashion,
true love will never die, it's symbolic.
It's *everlasting*!

My True Love Divine

In search of my *True Love*,
my heavenly *Prince* who's truly *Divine*,
I seek to win his heart
and won't stop until he's mine.

My heart is burning with desire,
I yearn for his touch.
I want to kiss him,
make love to him,
my body is calling out
for the warmth of his gentle touch.

I will patiently wait
til' the day he's by my side,
when he embrace me in his arms,
when I happily become his bride.

My Wish Would Be

With each passing day that you're not here
I sit and wonder where you are?

I often daydream and marvel
how our lives would be
if I made *just one wish* upon a star,
My wish would be...

That our lives be filled with love
and contentment,
no more pain or sorrow.
Enjoying the fruits of our labor
for a much brighter tomorrow.

To stop the clock
and turn back the hands of time,
back to the moment when we first met,
the day I longed for you to be mine.

To retract any wrongful thing
I've ever said or done.
To fill your heart with laughter,
leaving you to smile as bright
as the morning sun.

Your smile would be so bright
for all the world to see,
if I could make *just one wish*,
My wish would be...

For you to self-reflect
and see yourself as I do,
as a proud and intelligent man
excelling in all that you do.

Someone who will never allow
anyone to tamper with his pride,

it's what defines your true values,
your true character, it's who you are inside.

For you to understand
the difference between fact and fiction,
to never be fooled by lies
or someone's wrongful depiction
of whom they say they are,
which is probably not your friend;
someone you never should've trusted
only to realize it in a sad and bitter end.

For you to feel the same love
I feel for you, deep within my heart.
For you to feel the same pain I do
whenever we're apart.

For you to accept that my love for you is real,
there's nothing fake or phony about it
'cause it's truly how I feel.

For you to undoubtedly see
past the drama and all the lies,
to see my inner beauty,
who I really am inside.

For you to believe
that time will heal a broken heart,
because the truth of the matter is
"It wasn't I who tore us apart."
So, if I could make *just one wish*,
My wish would be…

For you to get past the confusion,
agony and illusion
by separating the twisted lies.
Learn how to compartmentalize
how you really feel,
then you will be able to believe in love,
our love and know that it's for real.

I make these wishes
because I want you to know
how special you are to me.

You have a heart of gold,
passion for succeeding
and a dynamic charm for all to envy.
You are my *Rock*, my *Salvation*,
you're the better half of me.
'*For a Lifetime of Love*,'
is what my wish would be.

So please...
Make all my wishes come true.

Patiently I Wait

You came into my life
and turned it upside down.
Leaving my head spinning,
constantly going round and round.

My mind is so bewildered,
I don't know if you're coming or going.
I asked myself over and over,
"What on earth is he doing?"

You have a beautiful woman
who loves you dearly,
yet you ponder your decision
by acting so weary.

Afraid to take a chance
to follow your fate,
even though you're lost and confused,
patiently I wait
for you to come to your senses
and open your eyes,
no longer living in darkness
of secrets and lies.

We are a perfect match,
an identical pair;
to abandon my love for you,
I will not dare.

Our future is destined by fate,
to live our lives together
as each other's soul-mate.

We are one step closer
for our special day to come,
when our hearts bond together
creating a perfect union.

Surrender to Love

To you I promise…
Not to look back over the years
as a mistake to regret.

I am stronger and wiser
and I'm ready to open my heart for the next
experience to come, which is now here with you,
to share in unconditional love,
being honest and faithful in all that I do.

To you I promise…
To surrender to your love
by allowing my past to be my guide,
I promise not to repeat the same mistakes
and put old differences aside.

Each day will be a lesson learned,
communication is the key;
through daily encouragement,
being positive and living our lives
in perfect harmony.

A solid foundation we will build,
reinforcing it every day;
by reassuring our love for one another
through many means and different ways.

Let us promise to never bring negativity
in to our happy home,
'cause when we do
it will lead to unhappiness,
leaving us all alone.

Why Do I Love Thee

Why do I love thee?
I've asked myself this question
a thousand times.

I love thee for his remarkable gifts,
one who is truly divine.
I love thee for his unselfish spirit,
the uniqueness of his soul.
The proud stance he has about himself
which defines strength for all that is bold.

When he offered me his broken heart
to mend with love and tender care,
I never took his love for granted,
I never will.
Do I dare!?

Dare to change what I know is fate,
uniting our souls to become one.
Joined together by the love we share,
creating a harmonious union.

Wishing You Were Here

So serene, all is green.
The sky is blue, something new.
I'm at the top, I made it here;
beautiful scenery, all is clear.

It was time to get away
from all my chores,
to enjoy the sites
of the great outdoors.

It's been a long hike,
bout' an hour or so,
gotta' make it downhill,
gotta' take on some mo'.

I'm glad I had a chance
to finally get away,
to break away from the routine
of my stressful days.

My company is good,
he's very nice.
Yet I'm juggling mixed emotions,
I don't want to have to slice
my feelings in two,
to choose between him or you?

I wish you were here,
my heart aches;
oh how I long to have you near.

I harbor your love deep within my soul.
You invigorate my spirit
by making me whole.

My heart feels uneasy,
my mind can't rest. In the end,
we would have proven our best.

That our love is everlasting
and can stand the test of time.
I will weather any storm
until you are mine.

I leave you with these special words
that are near and dear to my heart,
"My life is incomplete
when our souls are apart."

Until that day arrives
And your Spirit is near,
I will keep on wishing,
"Wishing you were here."

Woman of Beauty

My smooth bronze skin
glistens amidst the golden sand.
Your feet worn from your long journey,
crossing many seas and distant land.

You seek a woman of beauty,
more beautiful than the most elegant *Black Rose*.
My beauty is worth every step you traveled,
crossing turbulent seas and jagged roads.

Amazed to see such striking beauty
sparkle before your eyes;
to see *me* standing before you,
stunned to your surprise.

Your lonely heart begins to race,
as you gently caress
my beautiful face.

Our soft lips meet,
to share in a passionate kiss.
The intense energy from your spirit
reveals how much I've been missed.

You share exciting tales of your journey;
crossing roaring seas and distant land,
in search of your *Nubian Queen*
to be reunited with her with man.

As your *Queen,* you vow to worship me
with love and affection. To always worship
the radiance of my beauty as it glows; flawless.
A monument of *perfection!*

You are the Air I Breathe

I'm writing you this poem because I want you to know,
"You are the air I breathe, nothing else matters."
To go on living without you,
my whole world is shattered.

There's nothing more meaningful to me
in this world, than knowing that I'm
your one and only girl.

These past few years of loving you
has brought joy back into my life.
Loving you brings me serenity,
no more arguing, no more strife.

I often daydream of our future together,
when you're my husband and I'm your wife.
You've shown me love, you rescued me from pain,
I never thought I could ever love again.

Without you, my whole world is shattered.
Without you, nothing else matters.
To live without you;
tormented by misery and pain,
I'm just an empty soul
who can never love again.

With you, I'll be...
With you, I'm free...
Free to love...
Free to be...
Who you want me to be.

Your friend, your companion,
your lover, your wife.
Forever in your life.
You are the air I breathe, nothing else matters.

Your Silent Whisper

I sit alone
With thoughts of you on my mind.
Patiently waiting, allowing you time
To heal old wounds
From a once broken heart.
Sitting here pondering,
Alone in the dark.

Asking myself…
Does he miss me?
Does he love me?
Does he call out my name?
Only the sound of *your silent whisper*
Can ignite my internal flame.

The flame of our love
Burns deep within my heart.
The days are longer,
Stretched so far apart.
The nights are lonely,
Wishing you were here by my side;
I'll keep the flame burning,
I will keep it alive.

I sit still and ponder,
Now I brokenhearted.
What lead to this,
My dearly departed.
Lead you astray,
Away from me.
How could this be?

I say again…
Does he miss me?
Does he love me?
Does he call out my name?
Only the sound of *your silent whisper*
Can ignite my flame.

Haikus

Away from Home

A long kiss goodbye,
Gets us through the lonely nights,
Soon I will return home.

Forever in Love

Forever here to stay,
Never will I go away,
I will always love you.

Lonely Heart

Her mouth speak no words,
Her expressions shows her fear,
She cries in the night.

Romantic Vacation

Exotic beaches,
Glistening golden sands,
We walk hand in hand.

Sexy Lingerie

Gold, shimmer, sleek, smooth,
Satiny; elegantly
Draping my body.

Shipwrecked

The ship sailed away,
Sailed into the roaring seas,
Dreary night falls gloom.

Southern Comfort

Autumn leaves fall down,
A copper glow on the ground,
Soon will be winter.

Sunny Day

Laughter, joy and smiles,
Cheery, colorful and bright
Rainbow in the sky.

The Rainbow

Vibrant, Colorful,
Red, Yellow, Blue, Indigo
Seen through my window pane.

Unity of Love

She said she love him,
He made her very happy,
So she married him.

Wintertime

Cold, icy and wet,
Weighing down branches on trees,
A stormy winter's night.

Wondering Soul

Pain, a broken heart,
Agony from a sad life,
She is lost and confused.

Black Heaven
Erotica

Baby Close Your Eyes

Baby close your eyes,
tell me what you see?
Relax your mind
and get ready for me.

I wanna' take you there,
to a place you've never been.
I promise to take it slow
as I work my way in.

I wanna' get you in the mood,
so get ready to groove.
I wanna' set your body on fire,
have you ready to explode;
your juices will put out the flames,
I'll keep ya' beggin' for mo.'

I promise to take my time
as we slowly *bump and grind*.
I'll give you what ya' want,
satisfaction guarantee;
when I'm up in side ya'
I'll give you all of me.

So hold on tight to the sheets,
don't let them go;
anchor your body just right
as I take it nice and slow.

'Cause you'll be yearnin'
as our bodies be squirmin',
all night long you'll be whinin'
as I'm steady bumpin' and grindin'.

No more dreamin',
'cause you'll be screamin',
when I take you to ecstasy
you'll be beggin' for mo' of me!

So baby close your eyes,
tell me what you see?

Black Heaven

Relax for a moment,
close your eyes.
Take in a deep breath…

While inhaling slowly,
clear your mind of all your thoughts
and begin to fantasize,
about a place…

Now exhale…
Softly whisper my name
saying, *Sy' (sigh)*…
With a pleasingly smile upon your face.

This place,
is full of erotic treasures
that will tantalize your soul.
It's filled with youthful inspirations,
never a fear of growing old.

This place,
will enlighten your spirit
and will forever soothe your mind.
It's like no place ever traveled on earth
or ever built by mankind.

This place,
is unique like my name,
never visited or explored.
It's filled with sensual pleasures,
waiting for only you to adore.

Once you are there
there's no turning back,
are you ready to embark
upon this erotic journey
into the *Heavens* that are *Black*?

Black Heaven is a place
for *Black Kings* and *Black Queens*,
throne rulers of our destiny,
true believers of our faith;
majesties of our kingdoms,
who'll forever worship our mates.

There's no measure to our love,
it's to infinity, 'til the end of time.
Are you ready to embark upon
this erotic journey
into the *Black Heavens*,
are you ready to be mine?

Have you ever imagined us together,
perhaps as husband and wife?
I have, from the moment I first met you
when you walked into my life.

I knew things would be different,
my life as I once knew it
would never be the same.
My thoughts, my feelings,
my entire life has changed.

Each time we're together
our hearts spontaneously ignite with chemistry,
creating a burst of explosion of true love;
sending our souls in flight
to soar the *Black Heavens* above.

Your energy is felt
whenever you are near,
you send chills up my spine
as you breathe softly into my ear.

The welcoming touch of your strong hands
firmly caress my voluptuous hips.
The smoothness of your gentle tongue
glides seductively along my tender lips.

A lock from the curls of my hair,
you remove from my angelic face;
in the heat of erotic ecstasy
I fall into your warm embrace.

As we make passionate love,
you cradle my body onto the bed;
between the peaks of my succulent breasts,
gently I place your head.

You begin pleasing me, kissing me
from one nipple to the next;
wanting to feel you inside me
I become arousingly wet.

The warm juices from my vulva
oozes down my inner thighs,
the aroma of my sweet nectar
becomes intoxicatingly high.

Responding to my fervent desire,
intensely you draw me near;
the moment we've both been waiting for
is finally here.

Held enduringly in your warm embrace,
never wanting to let you go;
the tender love we make,
our bodies grindin' nice and slow.

As our bodies rejoice in a love song
of smooth melodies,
creating erotic rhythms from our moves;
our sensual passion is so instrumental
as we *whine* to a lustful groove.

We've fulfilled our fantasies,
an erotic journey of true love,
heated by your desire for tantalizing pleasure,
you've reached the *Black Heavens* above;
there's no turning back!

I say again,
"Are you ready for a new life
to enjoy and embrace
the Heavens that are *Black?*"

Black Panther

The sleek and sultry *Black Panther*
is lurking, seeking to devour his next prey.
Mesmerized by my scent,
drives him to quench his thirst my way.

He groans and moans as he sniffs the air
like a savoring *cat* in heat,
as he smells the aroma of my sweet nectar,
will I become his next prey to eat?

Cautiously he approaches me,
aroused by my defense,
he whispers softly into my ear,
"You summoned me with your scent."

Trembling by his presence,
slightly weakened by fear,
I too become aroused
the closer he draws near.

I begin to *purrrr* like a kitten,
staring deep into his dark eyes,
at that instant moment
I become mesmerized.

He carries me into his lair,
we make passionate love all night long,
our fervent bodies burn in ecstasy
until the break of dawn.

The *Black Panther* is feverish,
wanting me more and more.
He takes me as his *Queen,*
to forever worship, love and adore.

Breathless Anticipation

My ears should hear…
Soothing words,
Peaceful tones,
Reaffirmation of desire;
Breathless anticipation

My body should feel…
Knowing, probing,
Caressing fingers;
Firm, steady,
Approving hands;
Flexed-tightened muscles,
Soft lips, familiar and welcomed
In erogenous, sensitive
And excited regions;
Breathless anticipation

My eyes should see…
Amorous advance,
Yearning, longing,
Acknowledged eroticism;
Accepting intent,
Minimal clothing
Relinquished from a smooth,
Strong, muscular body;
Breathless anticipation

The atmosphere should be…
Light-starved with haunting,
Jazzy instrumental melodies
And warm misting steam,
White orchid lily aromatics
To accentuate my satisfaction.

"As you please me", she said,
"My pleasure!" Said he.

Day Dreamin' of You

It's been a long day at the office,
I'm winding down to the melodic sounds
of soothing-jazzy instrumentals.

Reclining back in my chair,
I begin to adjust myself,
I close my eyes to
thoughts are of you...

I arrive home,
upon entering the front door
I'm greeted with the aromatic fragrance
of a savory *Italian* meal.
Hmmm, as I begin salivating,
wondering, "What's for dessert?"

After putting down my briefcase,
I noticed a trail of rose pedals
spread throughout the carpet,
leading upstairs to the bedroom.

My curiosity is peaked
so I began to follow the pedals
into the bedroom,
leading to the bathroom door.

I approach a dimly lit room
infused with the fragrance
of lavender scented candles,
I stand quietly, watching you.

Instantly, I'm mesmerized
by your sexy, toned- *Nubian* body,
relaxing seductively
in a hot-steamy, foamy bath.

I watch as your inviting tongue
slowly trace the outer rim of a glass of *red wine,*

while peacefully grooving
to the harmonic sounds of *Najee'*,
I become hypnotized!

I'm aroused as your smooth, bronze body
become enveloped in a tub of rich, creamy,
vanilla-scented foam; as it hugs every inch
of your luscious curves.

Your head is tilted back
on an white *Egyptian-cotton* towel.
A few locks of your hair are suspended
in the soft glow of the candlelight.

I approach you to offer you a rub,
your eyes respond with seduction;
the inviting look upon your face
welcomes my harden loins.

Wanting...
Waiting...
Anticipating...
Penetration!

I respond to your request
by slowly discarding my clothes.
Standing before you- naked,
I accept the invitation to join you
in the hot-steamy, foamy bath.

Suddenly, I'm awakened
by the vibration in my pocket.
It's a text message:
"Baby I'm home, *Italian* for dinner…
A special surprise for dessert!"

I text you back:
"Keep the water hot baby, I'm on my way!"

First Glance

From a sudden glance our eyes meet,
reality lost, we become suspended in time.
Your curiosity's piqued, your senses heighten,
as your eyes gaze into mine.

Mesmerized by my seductive smile,
yearning to touch the smooth of my skin,
you're lovin' my style.

Captivated by the look of my bedroom eyes,
with thoughts of erotic desire,
you watch as I lick my lips softly with my tongue,
your temperature rise.

As your body is *warming,*
your muscles are *squirming,*
hoping to feel inside.

Aroused by the curves of my hips,
my voluptuous lips,
slowly you begin to close your eyes.

You have thoughts of caressing my body,
reaching heights of sensual pleasure,
you begin to *fantasize...*

Arisen by my spirit that moves you,
my body's rhythm that grooves you,
has your mind going insane.

You imagine me whispering:

Tease me...   *Taunt me...*   *Want me...*
Feel me...   *Taste me...*   *Kiss me...*
Lick me...   *Suck me...*   *Please me...*

As I'm screamin' your name!

Responding to the request
of your erotic desire,
heated by burning passion
which sets our souls on fire.

In a dark corner of the room,
one hand caresses my breast;
while sliding the other,
touching beneath my dress.

Parting my lips slowly to stick inside,
you get down on your knees
as I start to guide
your succulent tongue
between my thighs.

Exciting my juices the temptation rise,
the tip of your head you place inside;
gently it's welcomed as it slips and slide.
Aroused with passion the harder you thrust,
satisfying the ecstasy of our feverish lust.

Awaken!
Interrupted by the music that soothes the air,
I gaze into your eyes with affirmation
to take you there!

Got Me Goin' Crazy

The touch of your hands
Weaken my knees,
Got me sayin,'
"Baby... Baby... Baby... Please!"

So turn off the lights
And groove me some more,
Give me what I've been missing
And waiting for more.

More of...
The *feel* of you,
The *taste* of you,
The *want* of you...
Got me goin' crazy for more of you.

You excite regions in my body
That's never been explored,
Taking me to ecstasy
And wanting you more.

More of...
The *feel* of you,
The *taste* of you,
The *want* of you...
Got me goin' crazy for more of you.

So Baby please me tonight,
Do me up right,
Give me what I've been missing,
Love me just right.

Give me more of...
The *feel* of you,
The *taste* of you,
The *want* of you...
Got me goin' crazy for more of you.

I Often Fantasize

With each passing day that goes by,
I often fantasize, "If you were here by my side,
What's the first thing I would do, to you?"

My first thoughts take me back to the day
When you greeted me at your front door, naked.
Wearing an alluring smile on your face.

I stood there
Motionless,
Speechless.

I was aroused by the sight
Of your sweet tender body,
As it glistened adoringly
In the sunlight.

Oh, how the sunrays captured every inch
Of your voluptuous curves,
I had to pinch myself and questioned,
"What did I do to deserve
Such an erotic greeting at your front door?"

Standing there
Motionless,
Speechless,
My curiosity wanted more!

You reached down for the towel
That had fallen to the floor,
Staring up into my eyes
Then down to my pants,
Astound to your surprise
You were bewildered by my stance.

I remained
Motionless,
Speechless.

Watching you retrieve the towel
That had fallen to the floor,
My curiosity was never satisfied
'Til this day *I often fantasize,*
"If I would've reached for the towel,
Would I have gotten more?"

I Often Fantasize II

You extend me a second invitation to your place.
Minutes after my arrival, I'm greeted
with a delightful smile upon your face.
This time you're wearing a red silky camisole.

I stood there
Motionless,
Speechless,
Saying nothing at all.

Startled by the seductive look
In your pretty brown eyes,
I glanced down at my pants
And notice a rise!

As *it* stood firm at attention,
Demonstrated by my stance,
I pinched myself back into reality
To be released from this sudden trance.
My arms reach for you to turn you around,
Embracing your sexy, toned and tender body
I guide you down, to the floor.

Lying you on a soft leopard-skinned rug,
Holding you tightly, extending the hug.
Caressing you firmly in my arms,
Your hot body next to mine,
The rhythmic movement of our bodies
Dances in cadence, perfect harmony,
As we begin to *grind*.

I gently bit the crook of your neck,
You respond by groping my now harden *stick*.
I gradually trace my fingers along your inner thighs,
You begin to thrust your body forward...
Wanting me, accepting me,
Anticipating me inside!

I lick the sweet nectar of your juices,
Pouring from your pulsating lips.
I remove your black-laced panties
Just below your hips.

My salivating tongue
makes its way upward
Towards your voluptuous breast.

I caress them,
Suckle them,
And gently begin to kiss
Each nipple- feverishly,
Passionately, one at a time.

My heart is agonizing,
Dying to be inside you,
I'm losin' my mind.

The response of your body,
Wanting me,
Accepting me,
Asking for more,
I thrust myself- ready to enter you...

Suddenly, I hear the sound
Of your sweet voice
As you open the door,
You welcome me with but a polite *hello*.

I Often Fantasize III

Hearing the smooth sound
Of your rich velvety voice,
Tattoos erotic rhythms
On my heart.

Feeling the warm touch
Of your firm hands,
Holding me tightly in your arms,
Energizes my spirit.

You excite regions
Long since felt by a man's touch,
Or enchanted by the masculine fragrance
Of a man's scent.

Arousing my feminine loins,
I'm dripping wet.

Your scent, your touch,
Stiffens my nipples;
My full- round and inviting breast,
Anticipating your full lips, puckered;
Ready to envelope all of me.

No words are exchanged between us,
As I stare into the dark pools
Of your intriguing eyes,
I'm hypnotized.

Lifeless, like a feather amidst the wind,
Searching aimlessly for its wing,
I'm taken to a world filled with erotic treasures,
Where you pleasure me, and I pleasure you.

Is this seductive pool of eroticism, love
Or just my imagination?
I'm roused by a gentle kiss you place upon my cheek…

Inside You

Soft

    Wet

        Warm

            Velvet

                Beautiful

                    Juicy

                        Delicious…

Salivating

    Dripping

        Gushing

            Drowning

                Swollen

                    Belly Heaving

                        Intoxicating…

Deep

    Throbbing

        Penetration

            Release

                Explosion

                    Orgasmic

                    Ecstasy

                      Black Heaven!

Longing Desire

Velvety smooth, your skin,
the soft feel of rose pedals
dancing across my face.

Your aromatic scent of warm-vanilla musk
spontaneously ignites my erogenous zones,
from regions long since neglected.

My body yearns for the feel
of you warm, sensual touch.

Excited by the possibility
of exploring every inch of you.
Will you have me?

Smooth and Sexy Love

Girl you make me smile,
Come stay for a while;
Tickle my fancy
With your platinum treats.
Your smooth chocolate center,
Smellin' and tastin' so sweet.

I wanna take off all your clothes
'Cause you make me wanna eat
Your wet and tasty, *Smooth and Sexy Love,*
You're all I ever think of.

Let's capture the moment,
Allow me to savor the taste
Of your rich creamy filling,
Waiting for me to embrace
Your smooth chocolate center,
Smellin' and tastin' so sweet.

I want to take off all your clothes,
You make me wanna eat
Your wet and tasty, *Smooth and Sexy Love,*
You're all I ever think of.

You're my chocolate delight,
My rich creamy truffles,
Let's pull back the satin sheets
With fancy ruffles.

Satisfy my craving, fulfill my every desire
Of wanting your deep chocolate center,
Girl you set my soul on fire.

I need a taste of your
Smooth and Sexy Love,
Smellin' and tastin' so sweet.

Sweet Dreams of Ecstasy

As I lay my head down to rest
I pray to dream a thousand dreams,
In hopes to awaken to your tender lips,
Kissing me softly below my hips.

Rubbing your hand between my thighs,
You part my clit to lick inside;
Tasting the sweet nectar of my forbidden fruit;
Wetting my vulva, releasing my juice.

Your tongue glides softly, it doesn't hurt,
Inside your mouth I begin to squirt.
While moaning and groaning, I scream your name,
Saying, "Baby please take me, I'm going insane."

Like never before,
I've reached climax;
My body is trembling,
I'm shaking, I can't relax.

You place my arms above my head,
Inside my walls, you place the tip of *your*...
Now hardened, ready to please,
Guided in so gently, you start to tease.
I begin to accept it, deeper inside,
From the feel of my walls- the harder it rise.

I squeeze, you moan,
In rhythm we groove;
Your body is *whinin'*,
 I'm lovin' your moves.

With each passionate stroke
I glance upon your face,
Beyond the stars and heavens
You've reached a place
Filled with ecstasy, excitement,
And passionate love;

Your body is trembling
From the joys of our love.

Sy'... Oh *Sy'*...
As you scream my name,
Reaching *your* ultimate climax,
I awake from my dream.

Sweet Torture

Sweet Torture,
You exist just beyond my reach.
Your aroma is so intoxicating,
I can barely breathe.

Sweet Torture,
When I think of you,
I'm lost for words,
I don't know what to say.
Even though I can't enjoy all of you,
I think of you each day.

Sweet Torture,
When I think of the first time we met,
many decades ago,
our fond memories are hard to let go.

Sweet Torture,
When I see your smile,
your Spirit beckons me,
drawing me to the warmth of your embrace.
You caress me in your arms,
blowing soothing kisses upon my face.

Sweet Torture,
It hurts my soul to see others enjoy you
when I see their sails go by.
Not able to smell you,
feel you or enjoy you,
I would rather die!

Sweet Torture,
The jealously within my heart
fuels my every desire to have you.
Will that day ever come
when there's no more walls
or distance between us?

The day my heart succumbs;
The day I surrender to your beauty;
The day I hold you and never let you go;
The day these *prison walls* come tumbling down;
The day I walk across your shore.

Sweet Torture,
Until that day arrives
I will always dream of you.
To me you represent *Freedom,*
I will always love you!

Sweet Torture,
Sweet Torture,
Sweet Torture.

Tasty, Savory - Chocolate Treats

Creamy, sexy and silky smooth;
savory, delightful for any mood.

Elegant, seductive and pleasingly sweet,
taste of rich dark chocolate, decadent treats.

Capture the moment and savor the taste
of my rich creamy fillings,
waiting for you to embrace.

A mouthful of robust flavors,
filled with exotic treasures;
satisfying the desire
of my most erotic pleasures.

Fantasize no more,
allow me to tickle your fancy
with my platinum treats.

Rich caramels, creamy truffles
and delightful pralines;
your mouth will enjoy
all of my *savory* treats.

Tell Me What You Like

Tell me what *you* like,
Tell me what your *lips* like,
Tell me what your *tongue* like,
Tell me...
What do you like?

Do you like it like this,
Or do you like that?
Tell me...
What do you like?

I like it when your tongue
Traces the outline of my lips.
I like the way your tongue
Teasingly makes its way
Parting my full lips.

As it glides across my tongue
Towards my throat,
As it penetrates my mouth
The warmth of my saliva
Invites your tongue
To absorb all my wetness!

Now tell me...
Tell me what you like,
Tell me what your *lips* like,
Tell me what your *tongue* like,
Tell me...
What do you like?

The Feel of You

The touch of your gentle hands
Feels like brisk air
That excites my nipples.
When you caress me
I'm weakened,
My body is crippled.

Just to feel the warmth of your touch…
The feel of you,
The taste of you,
The want of you;

No wonder you have women
Waiting in line
Just to get a feel of you.

You tantalize my curiosity,
I want you so much!
My "Big Daddy"
Who's here to please me.

You have my heart doing a jig,
Making up its own dance.
You got me waiting in line
For my next chance,

At getting
A feel of you,
A taste of you,
All of you!

No wonder you have women
Waiting in line
Just to get a feel of you.

The Kiss

Fullness, embodied,
Wet, juicy,
Savory, tasteful,
Luscious, succulent,
Gentle, passionate.

Teasingly soft,
Two lips connecting,
Shared emotions;
Initiating possibilities,
Temptations of hope.

The sun and moon smiling,
Shaking hands;
Shooting stars victory dance
As they twinkle brighter.

Words reduced to feelings,
Rejoiced emotions,
Initiating lead;
Warm embrace,
Beginning introduction.

Seductive,
Long,
Anticipated,
Kiss!

The Way You Make Me Feel

From the glow of your smile,
To the touch of your hands,
It's something bout
The way you make me feel .

Together there's chemistry,
There is no mystery
In the way you make me feel.

When you touch me from head to toe,
There's no place you'll never go,
In the way you make me feel.

You light my fire with melting desire,
I got to have more of you,
There's nothing I'll never do
'Cause of the way you make me feel.

You take me to limits I've never been,
In the pit of my soul I feel you within,
I gotta have more of you;
There's nothing I'll never do
'Cause of the way you make me feel.

So bring back that feeling,
Touch me from head to toe,
There's no place you'll never go
In the way you make me feel.

ABOUT THE AUTHOR

Syneeda "Sy" Penland was born and raised in the suburbs just north east of Atlanta Georgia, post-civil rights era. Growing up the youngest of four children in an underprivileged, mixed race community, Sy's mother sheltered her from bigotry and hate; while single-handedly raising four children. As a young girl, Sy didn't need much to make her happy besides a book, a pen or pencil, and a note-book journal. These items were just as valuable to her over a new doll, a new bicycle or a new pair of roller skates; which she enjoyed as a child. The more books she read, the more Sy fantasized about becoming one of the many characters she'd read about.

Early on in her childhood, she would day-dream about leaving home to travel to exotic places around the world. Before joining the Navy, Sy' was able to live out some of her fantasies through her poetry. A few weeks after graduating high school she vowed to leave the confines of her small town to make a better life for herself, in hopes of becoming a famous writer or news journalist. This journey first took her to Los Angeles in the summer of 1989 to live with her aunt.

Unfortunately it only took a few months for Sy' to realize that her Aunt was just a strict and stern as her mother and grandmother, thereby prohibiting Sy' to vastly explore her true talents as a naturally gifted writer. Sy' briefly returned back to her roots; within a few weeks she was off again. This is when she decided to join the Navy, in search of a new adventure in life.

For the next 20 years of her Navy career, while first serving as an enlisted sailor, and later as a senior Naval Officer, Sy' battled adversity. Be it ongoing racism, sexism or other unlawful and unethical acts of discrimination. Towards the end of her military career, Sy' turned to her natural gift to find her true identity and her true voice. While facing many trials and tribulations in the wake of later becoming a military whistleblower, Sy' was able to use one of her many gifts to *"Self-Reflect"* upon her life's journey. While writing this remarkable collection, she became many characters, ideas, thoughts and reality. This time in her own life.

Syneeda is often referred to as a *reincarnated* old soul, who speaks truth of our past, present and future. When it comes to confronting race related issues, Sy' sees no color, only truth. She hopes her collection will help to open the eyes, minds and hearts of others so they can accept the reality of "truth". Thereby conditioning their minds to love one another without fear of racial prejudice and their willingness to receive love, no matter what!

It is within the depth of my soul that I righteously believe, "Speaking truth to bring internal peace in one's life is a moral win that cannot be measured in court or by the eyes of man."

As a human rights activist, author, poet and songwriter, Syneeda's dream is to one day collaborate with other artists, spiritual groups and organizations in helping to spread God's inspirational seeds: "messages of hope, peace, love, happiness and unity", throughout the world. She believes that by working together in perfect harmony, is when we can truly experience God's unselfish love, peace and joy for all of humanity!

www.ingramcontent.com/pod-product-compliance
Lightning Source LLC
Chambersburg PA
CBHW031301090426
42742CB00007B/555